Freedom

S. R. Maggs

S. R. MAGGS

Copyright © 2018 S. R. Maggs

ISBN-13: 978-1790-9-4257-2

FREEDOM

For Freedom.

FREEDOM

You take advantage of freedom. You abuse her, test her, and forget her. But yet she's still there when you rest at night and wake in the morning.

Freedom is still by your side, knowing you need her. Knowing you love her.

When freedom is taken from you, you realize how much you miss her, but you are the one to blame. It's your fault, your fault for committing a crime.

Yet, you blame others. You are the one who decides how to act. You are the one who's responsible for your actions, no one else is. Saying otherwise is cowardice. You are not the victim.

The prison has a distinct scent, a scent that is now yours. That is the smell of stale darkness you have now adopted from forfeiting your freedom.

It is then when you realize how much freedom provided you without expecting anything in return, without sending you a bill of the debt you owe her. Those in camo, in blue, and their families are the ones who have picked up the check. What you have forgotten to do is pay her respect, so she can no longer confide in you.

The bitter cold and unbearable heat fluctuates the cells, with no hint of privacy or individuality. You now belong to the system and the inmates that use you for survival. It's not family in there, it's only survival. Thus, human nature prevails.

15

The stares from other inmates look cold and empty, but full of evil. Soon yours will be the same.

17

The unfortunate truth about your new home is that it becomes your norm. Its values are now your values. As long as you serve your time, it is your reality.

Any attempt to transition to the outside becomes futile, because the outside is now the foreign land, and you would fail to adapt to how life used to be. You'd soon long to return to the prison smell, the minuscule cells, and the inmate tribe, even if doing so means death.

21

So, before you make decisions that strip away your freedom, take a look around. Feel the nourishment, the hope, and the love. Don't ever lose sight that freedom sets these on the table for you.

23

Thus, be careful, as your actions could spiral into another world, another norm, and another reality far away from freedom. Nothing is worth losing her.